Catholic Update
guide to
Vatican II

MARY CAROL KENDZIA,
Series Editor

Franciscan
MEDIA
Cincinnati, Ohio

RESCRIPT
In accord with the *Code of Canon Law*, I hereby grant my *Imprimatur*
the *Catholic Update Guide to Vatican II.*

Vicar General and Auxiliary Bishop
of the Archdiocese of Cincinnati
Cincinnati, Ohio
August 24, 2012

The *Imprimatur* ("Permission to Publish") is a declaration that a book or pamphlet is considered to be free from doctrinal or moral error. It is not implied that those who have granted the *Imprimatur* agree with the contents, opinions or statements expressed.

Scripture passages have been taken from *New Revised Standard Version Bible,* copyright ©1989 by the Division of Christian Education of the National Council of the Churches of Christ in the U.S.A., and used by permission. All rights reserved.
Excerpts from the documents of Vatican II are adapted from the versions available at www.vatican.va.

Cover and book design by Mark Sullivan
Cover image © Fotolia | Oscity

LIBRARY OF CONGRESS CATALOGING-IN-PUBLICATION DATA
Catholic update guide to Vatican II / Mary Carol Kendzia, series editor.
p. cm. — (Catholic update guides)
Includes bibliographical references.
ISBN 978-1-61636-576-9 (alk. paper)
1. Vatican Council (2nd : 1962-1965) I. Kendzia, Mary Carol.
BX8301962 .C38 2012
268'.52—dc23

2012033659

ISBN 978-1-61636-576-9

Copyright ©2012, Franciscan Media. All rights reserved.
Published by Franciscan Media
28 W. Liberty St.
Cincinnati, OH 45202
www.FranciscanMedia.org

Printed in the United States of America.
Printed on acid-free paper.
12 13 14 15 16 5 4 3 2 1

Contents

About This Series

The Catholic Update guides take the best material from our best-selling newsletters and videos to bring you up-to-the-minute resources for your faith. Topically arranged for these books, the words you'll find in these pages are the same clear, concise, authoritative information you've come to expect from the nation's most trusted faith formation series. Plus, we've designed this series with a practical focus—giving the "what," "why," and "how to" for the people in the pews.

The series takes the topics most relevant to parish life—e.g., the Mass, sacraments, Scripture, the liturgical year—and draws them out in a fresh and straightforward way. The books can be read by individuals or used in a study group. They are an invaluable resource for sacramental preparation, RCIA participants, faith formation, and liturgical ministry training, and are a great tool for everyday Catholics who want to brush up on the basics.

The content for the series comes from noted authors such as Thomas Richstatter, O.F.M., Lawrence Mick, Leonard Foley, O.F.M., Carol Luebering, William H. Shannon, and others. Their theology and approach is grounded in Catholic practice and tradition, while mindful of current Church practice and teaching. We blend each author's style and approach into a voice that is clear, unified, and eminently readable.

Enrich your knowledge and practice of the Catholic faith with the helpful topics in the Catholic Update Guide series.

Mary Carol Kendzia
Series Editor

Introduction

On October 11, 2012, the Church celebrated the fiftieth anniversary of Blessed Pope John XXIII opening the Second Vatican Council. Perhaps more than any other event in recent years, Vatican II can define a generation, an attitude, an outlook, an understanding of both the Church and the world, perhaps even an understanding of faith itself. Whether one regards it as positive or negative, the effect of the Council on Catholicism today cannot be denied.

On the thirtieth anniversary of the Council, Franciscan Fr. Leonard Foley made this observation:

> If you are thirty or younger, you have heard a thousand times: "You have no idea how it was back then, before Vatican II—Mass in Latin, priest with his back to you, no one else in the sanctuary except altar boys, no parish

councils, fasting from midnight (even from water) before Communion."

If you were thirty or so at the time, you probably didn't have much time, between kids and bills, to pay attention to what 2,500 bishops were doing over there in Rome. The idea of English in the liturgy seemed good, though. And if you were grandparents or older, you lived through "the changes"—perhaps with fear and bewilderment, perhaps with a secret delight that "by gosh, the Church does change after all!"

Some have forgotten Vatican II. There is a minority—who knows how large?—that is still appalled and sometimes bitter at what seems to them betrayal. Most Catholics, however, seem to have accepted the changes with good grace.

On the fortieth anniversary, Edward Hahnenberg, professor of theology at Xavier University, reflected on teaching Vatican II to college students:

I once mentioned Vatican II in class and a student in the back raised his hand to ask, "Why don't they call it Vatican One, like Air Force One?" This sincere undergraduate thought I was talking about the pope's airplane. When I began to explain that Vatican II was a worldwide gathering of Catholic bishops that took place in the early

1960s, his eyes glazed over as he muttered, "The Sixties? That's ancient history!"

Our world is changing at an even faster pace than it did in the whirlwind 1960s. One of the gifts the Church offers us is being rooted in a history and a tradition that is "ever ancient, ever new." The spirit of the Second Vatican Council is very much a part of the Church today as we continue to explore the implications of its teachings.

CHAPTER ONE

The World of Vatican II

The Second Vatican Council (1962–1965) was one of the great moments in the history of our Church. It marked a time when the Church took a look at where it was and where the world was—and sought to close the gap. The Council wasn't a sudden event; years of changes in the world and years of study among Church leaders and theologians brought us all to this great moment.

Although Pope John XXIII (1958–1963) is rightly given credit for initiating the Second Vatican Council, the preparations for a council had been discussed for many years. But it was Pope John, a student of Church history with firsthand experience of the joys and troubles of the world, who brought the spirit of informed openness that so shaped Vatican II. And of course it is to the credit of his successor, Paul VI (1963–1978), that the Council moved forward following John's death.

It was the timing of that Council—the dawn of satellite communications—that suddenly put the Church in touch with more of the world. Evangelizing possibilities were now greater than ever; but now, too, the world could look in on the Church and challenge it.

It is important to consider the world into which Vatican II came. For half a century what has been called the greatest cultural change in the history of the world took place, at least in the West. Think of four inventions: the automobile, jet, radio, television. Now try to imagine what the world would have been like—would be like today—without them. Try to imagine the effect on your mind—mostly unconscious—of the speed in going from here to there, the effect on your mind of what can only be called an explosion of knowledge through radio and TV. We were flooded with fast-breaking news, with assertions, rumors, revelations, gossip, discoveries, entertainment—at the touch of a dial. We heard and saw history as it was happening. We learned of the foibles and sins of the high and mighty.

Into this roiling, questioning, learning, self-confident, self-doubting world marched Vatican II. Pope John XXIII, a simple "transitional" pope, was the knight in nothing but the armor of hope and joy who led the bishops. He hoped to open some windows, restore the Church's energy, and search for new forms best adapted to its present-day needs. The Church had to show itself alive and well amid the fog and noise. It had to lift its voice to the desperate world.

The theme of the Council was *aggiornamento*, which literally means "getting up to today." The Church was being urged to "update" itself.

In his opening speech to the Council, Pope John affirmed that the Church prefers "the medicine of mercy rather than of severity." The same Church, he adds, was to show herself "the loving mother of all, benign, patient, full of mercy and goodness towards the brethren who are separated from her." There were to be no condemnations, no anathemas.

The agenda of other councils, in earlier periods of history, had been determined by others—ranging from those who denied the divinity of Christ to those who denied the authority of Peter. It is understandable, in human disputes, that if you deny my position, I will respond by overemphasizing it. If I reject your point of view, you will hold to it more firmly and make it nearly essential. But as for all the things we agree on—they're forgotten.

For example, after the Protestant Reformation, the Catholic Church countered the ideas of the reformers with the Council of Trent (1545–1563). This Council defined certain doctrines the Protestants denied. Thus emphasized, these doctrines received an attention that outweighed others of greater importance.

On the other hand, things that were denounced by the reformers—indulgences, prayers to the saints, prayers for the dead—received disproportionate Catholic emphasis by way of reaction. Protestants emphasized the Bible; Catholics, tradition (thus, some Catholics edged away from using the Bible itself, getting instruction from sermons and catechisms, until Vatican II renewed interest in Scripture study).

Protestants denied the visible, juridical, hierarchical Church and opted for an invisible, internal, charismatic Church. So Catholics put primary emphasis on the Church being a hierarchically organized society. This imbalance lasted until Vatican II, when emphasis again was placed on the divine element in the Church.

It was as if the Church said at the start of Vatican II, "Come, let us sit down together and count our pluses, the common values we share. It's a rough world out there. We must be together and face all these problems together." Perhaps the most surprising fact some of us remember is that there were Protestant observers at the Council.

The Four Annual Sessions
The following is the barest outline of the doings of the Council. When you consider the sheer number of important documents discussed (sixteen)—not to speak of their own complex outlines—you can understand the immense amount of discussion, prayer, study—and, yes, argument—that went into four

years. For more than two thousand Church leaders to come to almost unanimous agreement on such a bewildering array of topics is almost tangible proof of the presence of the Spirit.

First Session (September–December, 1962). Attendance by bishops fluctuated during the four sessions: 2,908 bishops had a right to come, and 2,540 took part in the first session. They had submitted more than 8,000 suggestions to the preparatory committees.

On the very first day of the first session something happened that had permanent results. On the motion of Cardinal Lienart of France, the Council adjourned after a few minutes. The problem he raised was that there was not a diverse enough representation of various points of view on the various commissions. The result was that the memberships of these commissions were broadly expanded.

As could have been predicted, there were not many concrete results from the first session. Work already had begun on what would be the dominant concern—and the greatest achievement—of the Council: the Dogmatic Constitution on the Church.

The first session ended. The bishops went home to pray, study, and confer. During the nine-month interval, Pope John XXIII died on June 3, 1963. Cardinal Giovanni Montini, archbishop of Milan, was elected to the papacy June 21, 1963, becoming Pope Paul VI.

Second Session (September 29–December 4, 1963). At a public session, Pope Paul VI opened the second period of the Council with a memorable address in which he begged the pardon of non-Catholics for any fault Catholics may have for the divided state of Christianity. He also expressed the willingness of Catholics to forgive any injuries done to them.

In addition, the pope streamlined some of the Council procedures and announced an increase in the membership of each commission. Among the decisions of the Council during this session was that of including Mary in the document on the Church rather than giving her a separate document. This emphasized her vital relationship to the body of the faithful.

The principal achievement of this session was the approval of the Constitution on the Sacred Liturgy by a vote of 2,147 to 4. A lesser-known document, the Decree on the Means of Social Communication, also was passed.

The most dramatic conflict of the Council occurred when Cardinal Josef Frings, Archbishop of Cologne, frankly criticized the Holy Office (the Congregation for the Doctrine of the Faith), which prompted Cardinal Alfredo Ottaviani, then Secretary of the Holy Office, to defend it staunchly. During the interval between the second and third sessions, Pope Paul VI announced that women auditors (lay and religious) had been invited to the Council.

Third and Fourth Sessions (September 14–November 21, 1964, and September 14–December 8, 1965). Fourteen of the Council's sixteen documents were thoroughly discussed, revised, and finally approved during these two very busy and productive sessions. A list of their titles and dates of approval reveals the breadth and depth of the Council's deliberations and decisions:

The Constitution on the Sacred Liturgy (December 4, 1963)

Decree on the Means of Social Communication (December 4, 1963)

Dogmatic Constitution on the Church (November 21, 1964)

Decree on the Catholic Eastern Churches (November 21, 1964)

Decree on Ecumenism (November 21, 1964)

Decree on the Pastoral Office of Bishops in the Church (October 28, 1965)

Decree on the Up-to-Date Renewal of Religious Life (October 28, 1965)

Decree on the Training of Priests (October 28, 1965)

Declaration on Christian Education (October 28, 1965)

Declaration on the Relation of the Church to Non-Christian Religions (October 28, 1965)

Dogmatic Constitution on Divine Revelation (November 18, 1965)

Decree on the Apostolate of Lay People (November 18, 1965)

Declaration on Religious Liberty (December 7, 1965)

Decree on the Church's Missionary Activity (December 7, 1965)

Decree on the Ministry and Life of Priests (December 7, 1965)

Pastoral Constitution on the Church in the Modern World (December 7, 1965)

We will explore some of these documents in the last chapter.

Questions for Reflection

1. If you're over fifty, what are your memories of the years of the Council? If younger, what stories do you remember hearing about the changes?

2. A key phrase marking the need for a Second Vatican Council was *aggiornamento*, which means updating. Are there areas in the Church today that you feel need to be updated? Where and why?

3. What do you hope to gain from learning about Vatican II?

CHAPTER TWO

Trends of Vatican II

Most people have not read more than a few passages from the formal documents set forth by the Second Vatican Council. But every Catholic alive today has been influenced by the changes that came about in the life of the Church. In this chapter, we will join *Catholic Update* editor Jack Wintz, O.F.M., in looking at some key trends that emerged after the Council.

What Was New After Vatican II?

Dynamic Liturgies

Vatican II's Constitution on the Sacred Liturgy urges "full, conscious and active participation in liturgical celebrations" (14). The liturgical renewal that swept through the Church after Vatican II brought new life to the celebration of the Eucharist and other sacraments. New sacramental rites and the use of local languages encouraged more full and active participation.

Before Vatican II, the priest celebrated Mass in Latin with his back to the people, making the action of the Mass seem far away. It was easy for the faithful to fall into the role of spectators. Now the assembly is more actively engaged, helping us to experience "all of us" celebrating the Eucharist with the priest.

The Church now stresses the communal dimension of all the sacraments, seeing them as "community events," not private rituals. The Rite of Christian Initiation of Adults is a dramatic sign of this communal approach to the sacraments.

Before the RCIA was reestablished, the typical approach to adult baptism was isolated from the parish community. Preparation often consisted of around six weeks of private instructions followed by baptism on a Sunday afternoon, attended by a small cluster of relatives or friends.

Today, the RCIA process lasts a year or more and involves sponsors, catechists and, indeed, the whole parish. The sacraments of initiation—baptism, confirmation, and Eucharist—are celebrated within the context of community at the Easter Vigil. This communal spirit is also reflected in other sacraments.

The Laity

Laypersons are now recognized in a way surpassing anything in the past. "Everything that has been said about the People of God is addressed equally to laity, religious and clergy" (30). The laity are not, then, merely what is left over (99.99 percent) after the pope, the bishops, the priests, and the religious. "A secular character is proper and peculiar to the laity," and they "seek the kingdom of God by engaging in temporal affairs" (31). "There is a common dignity of members deriving from their rebirth in Christ, a common grace as sons and daughters, a common vocation to perfection" (32). Men and women of the laity are commissioned to their apostolates by the Lord himself, through baptism and confirmation. So they are a part of the Church's mission. They are not just "allowed to help."

In the chapter "The Call to Holiness," a most important principle is declared: "All Christians in any state or walk of life are called to the fullness of Christian life and to the perfection of love" (40). "The forms and tasks of life are many, but Holiness is one—that sanctity which is cultivated by all who act under God's Spirit" (41).

Do "ordinary" Catholics believe this, even today? That Joe and Ellen and Juan and Natasha are called to the same holiness as Pope John XXIII and contemplative nuns, parish priests, and missionaries in Africa? Some of the most astounding pronouncements of the Council are the simplest.

It's common today to see laypeople assisting at Mass as Eucharistic ministers. These and other liturgical ministers— ushers, greeters, lectors, and music ministers—are visible reminders of the wide variety of laypeople who minister within the Church. Some serve as catechists or youth ministers, others as hospital chaplains, bereavement ministers, administrators of priestless parishes, and outreach workers.

Behind this burgeoning lay involvement in ministry is the reality that more Catholics are embracing their baptismal call to ministry or service to the Church and, indeed, to the world at large.

At the same time that the role of the laity is growing, we are experiencing a decline in the number of ordained ministers. The Holy Spirit is clearly leading us to a more inclusive model of Church in which we recognize the need for both lay and ordained ministers to make the work of the Church complete.

Women are among those becoming more engaged in Church ministry today, though many believe their potential has not been fully realized. What full ministry for women should mean is a sensitive question requiring further discernment. Those awaiting greater acknowledgment in the Church also include ethnic minorities, Catholics with disabilities, and many others whose gifts have not yet been fully respected or utilized.

New Interest in Scripture

More Catholics are reading the Bible today—with more solid understanding—than at any other time in Church history.

Growing numbers of laypeople are attending theology schools, leading or joining Bible study groups, and reading an array of articles and books on the subject. Priests and vowed religious are no longer the only Scripture experts.

The Church today encourages its members to make use of new methods of Scripture study and to cherish the Scriptures. Catholics are growing in their understanding of the Bible through the benefits of historical research, literary analysis, and archaeological findings. Church documents wisely steer Catholics away from literal-minded approaches and from reading the Bible as if it were a science or history textbook.

Also of note is that, through the Lectionary's three-year cycle, Catholics are now exposed to a wider variety of Scripture readings at Sunday Mass. The use of Scripture readings has been enhanced in other sacramental rites as well.

As Catholics are nourished by the life-giving word of God, they become better instruments of evangelization and of the world's transformation.

Outreach to All Humanity

One of the most warmly received insights of Vatican II is that salvation is concerned not solely with saving souls but also with saving the whole person—body and soul. This holistic view is appealing because we naturally do not want to lose any genuine part of our human experience. St. Irenaeus, often quoted at the time of Vatican II, captured this well: "The glory of God is the human person fully alive!"

Jesus's mission on earth was not only to free the human heart from sin, but also to free men and women from disease, oppression, and everything that hinders their development as humans created by God and destined for eternal life. When we profess our belief in the resurrection of the body, this integral salvation is implied.

In The Church in the Modern World, the bishops of Vatican II acknowledged the intimate bond between the Church and all humanity. This great document begins: "The joys and hopes, the grief and anguish of the people of our time, especially those who are poor or afflicted, are the joys and hopes, the grief and anguish of the followers of Christ. Nothing that is genuinely human fails to find an echo in their hearts."

This conviction is evident in a new commitment to ecumenism as well as the acknowledgment of salvation outside of the Catholic Church (Dogmatic Constitution on the Church, 15–16). In addition to his many heroic firsts in the ecumenical effort, Pope John Paul II powerfully expressed this attitude during his first visit to the United States in October 1979. His first words were: "I want to greet all Americans without distinction. I want to tell everyone that the pope is your friend and a servant of your humanity."

Every authentic dimension of human existence is to be saved and brought to wholeness. As the pope's words suggest, we are to help all people come to their full humanity as men and women created in the image and likeness of God and redeemed by Christ.

Growth of Social Justice

Social justice has always been a crucial component of the Church's teaching and mission. Pope Leo XIII is sometimes credited with daring to be specific about what the Church has to say about particular social issues, though. And Vatican II extended that tradition.

In 1983, the bishops of the United States issued *The Challenge of Peace*, a pastoral letter on war and peace. In it they discussed the morality of war and of nuclear weapons. To help Catholics form their consciences on economic matters, they issued a pastoral letter on the U.S. economy in 1986. More recently, the U.S. bishops addressed civic responsibility in the document *Faithful Citizenship*.

Conscientious Catholics are reading these and other statements that the bishops have published on political and social issues. Church leaders continue to encourage Catholics to let their hearts be guided by the "social gospel."

Some people, however, are uncomfortable with the Church's involvement in public issues. They criticize the Church for "meddling in politics." Taking to heart the holistic view of salvation will help us see the mission of the Church as healing unjust political structures and laws as well as unjust hearts.

Martin Luther King, Jr., illustrated this point during a speech in 1964 when he said: "The law cannot make a man love me, but it can keep him from lynching me!" King helps us see that Christians must seek to transform not only sinful hearts but also the sinful laws and customs of society that oppress and dehumanize our sisters and brothers.

Catholic social teaching reminds us that it is not enough to passively await God's kingdom in the next life. We are also called to make that kingdom present now, by working as God's instruments to remove injustice, discrimination, poverty and disease from our midst.

Questions for Reflection

1. What change in the Church since Vatican II gives you the most encouragement about the Church's future?
2. Through baptism we are called to share in the ministry of the Church. In what ways do you live out this call to ministry? How can you become a more active member of the laity?
3. How does the Church's teaching on social issues affect your daily life?

CHAPTER THREE

Today's Church:
A Look in the Mirror

We will now take a closer look at the Dogmatic Constitution on the Church (*Lumen Gentium* or "Light to the Nations") because of its profound importance for our understanding of ourselves as Church today.

At first, this document might not seem exciting to anyone who expects new, wild, sensational changes in the Church. It begins very simply: "Christ is the light of humanity; and it is, accordingly, the heartfelt desire of this sacred Council…that…it may bring to all men and women the light of Christ which shines out visibly from the Church."

The Church, as described in this document, is not merely an institution, a bloc to be reckoned with. It is not a ticket to salvation once you get your name in the book and observe the minimum. It is not out to condemn, defeat, be Number One, put the fear of the Church militant into its enemies.

No, the Church is *a community that carries the light of Christ on its face*. What else is necessary? Some organization, surely. Some definite statement of principle. But to be a community shining like Jesus is at the heart of the Church's identity, say the Council fathers.

Impossible? Of course. Yet that is the Church's nature and task. It is as if the Church must say, embarrassedly, "Jesus is no longer visible, except sacramentally. We're sent to show you how he looked."

Jesus is not visible today: Therefore he must be seen in us— his radiance on our faces. This means we the Church are a sacrament. That is, there is something visible that reveals and hides a deeper reality. The external Church, like the human nature of Jesus, conceals and reveals the inner divine reality of the Church. (How sad, then, for those who dismiss the Church when they cannot see its inner beauty because of the sins of some of its members.)

Do we consider ourselves *primarily* a community and a sacrament to reveal Christ? Is that what Christians are? If we the Church do not think of ourselves that way, what might be the reason? Perhaps the following could be one explanation.

The Church is mystery/sacrament; partly human, partly

divine (Jesus is, after all, a member of the Church). We not only believe in (that is, as members of) the Church, we believe *in* the Church.

The order of treatment in the document is important: first, the mystery of the Church; second, the *People of God*—and only then the hierarchical distinctions. But the faithful altogether, *the whole people*, are seen as equal before God in baptism, though they might have various functions in the Church.

When you hear the word *Church*, does you think of the pope and his Vatican officials? Or do you think of the bishop and his diocesan staff? Or perhaps *Church* brings to mind your local pastor and the various ministers in your parish community. Is there another way of thinking about Church? Would it occur to you to put the question this way: What do *I* think about these issues? What do *my fellow parishioners* think about them? What do *Catholic people throughout the world* think about them? Are these also viable ways of understanding Church?

It is probably true to say that before Vatican II most people would have been satisfied to accept the first three ways of thinking about Church—as pope, bishop, or pastor—as adequate descriptions. These views represent a hierarchical way of seeing Church, a top-to-bottom view. What was revealed at the Council was a new vision of Church. At least it was new to most people at the time. It actually goes back to a very early, biblical perspective.

Vatican II's Vision of Church

Fundamental to Vatican II's vision is an emphasis on the Church as the People of God. True, the Church is a hierarchical community. Please note, though, that hierarchical is the adjective; community is the noun. Since nouns are more substantive than adjectives, it is fair to say community trumps hierarchy. While hierarchy is important, the community must come first.

Preceding any distinction between lay and ordained is the reality of Christian baptism. Baptism incorporates us all into an egalitarian community in which all are one and equal in Christ. A priest, bishop, or pope receives his Christian identity in the same way as all God's people: through baptism. As Cardinal Suenens said in a homily at a memorial Mass for Pope John XXIII, the most significant day in the life of a priest, bishop, or pope is not the day of his ordination but the day he was baptized into Christ Jesus.

Yves Congar, one of the theologians of the Council, wrote that it is not laypersons who have to define themselves in terms of their relation to the hierarchy but rather the hierarchy that needs to define itself in relation to the whole People of God. It is most importantly the People of God of whom they are a part and whom they are called upon to serve.

All the baptized are the People of God. All are called to build up the Church: the members of the hierarchy in their way, and the rest of the baptized in theirs. Giving priority to people fits well with the derivation of the Greek word used for Church in the New Testament—*ekklesia*. Its literal meaning is "those who are called together by God."

Church Buildings

Catholic church buildings might be called "churches" only in a derivative sense: They are not the Church, but the place where the Church, God's people, gathers. In ancient times a pagan temple was the house of a particular god. The priest alone entered the temple; people prayed outside. The same was true of the Jewish temple in Jerusalem: It was the house of God. People gathered in courts outside the temple, and only the priest was allowed to enter it.

A Catholic church is very different. It is not God's house; it is rather the place where God's people assemble. You don't need a building to have the Church. It is people, not bricks and mortar, that make up the Church.

Return to a Collegial Model

The Council also set out to decentralize the Church. It did this by emphasizing the unique importance of each local church. It made clear that each bishop is the vicar of Christ in the local church over which he presides: "The bishops, as vicars and legates of Christ, govern by their counsels, persuasion, and example the particular Churches assigned to them" (*Lumen*

Gentium, 27). The local bishop, therefore, is not primarily an agent of Rome but of the Holy Spirit.

This shift in focus meant a return to the principle of collegiality—so important in the first millennium of Christianity. Collegiality means that the Catholic bishops throughout the world, together with and under the leadership of the pope, possess supreme authority and pastoral responsibility for the whole Church. Besides the responsibilities they have in their local churches, bishops are called to have concern for the universal Church.

The First Vatican Council asserted that the pope was able to exercise supreme authority without consulting the bishops. The Second Vatican Council, without denying that the pope can exercise such authority, suggested—at least hinted—that perhaps he ought not do so. Before making any major statements, the pope would be well advised to consult with the bishops of the world so that what the Spirit is saying to the local churches can be incorporated into statements intended for the entire world.

The book of Revelation offers sound advice in this regard. In the letters addressed to the local churches in Asia, each concludes with a similar message: "Let anyone who has an ear listen to what the Spirit is saying to the churches" (Revelation 2:7).

Local Collegiality

But collegiality does not stop with the college of bishops. This principle needs to be extended to the local Church. If the bishop wants to be a good teacher whose teaching reaches the minds and hearts of his people, he also must be a good listener.

He needs to hear what priests, religious, and laity in his diocese are saying as they attempt to live out the gospel in their daily lives. When the bishop listens to them and incorporates their experiences into the teaching of the gospel, he will be better assured that his teaching will be vital as well as relevant.

The principle of collegiality deserves an even wider application. It also should find expression in the lives of the individual parishes in a diocese. After all, it is in their parish community that most Catholics experience the reality of Church. It is here they are baptized, confirmed, and celebrate the Eucharist. It is the place where they marry and where their children are baptized. It is with their fellow parishioners and their pastors that they share the joys and sorrows, the agonies and the ecstasies of life.

Pastors of parishes need to listen to the faithful in their parish: "The sacred pastors…should recognize and promote the dignity and responsibility of the laity in the Church. They should willingly use their prudent advice and confidently assign offices to them in the service of the Church, leaving them freedom and scope for activity. Indeed, they should encourage them to take on work on their own initiative" (*Lumen Gentium*, 37).

This should be especially true in areas where the laity have expertise their pastors lack. "To the extent of their knowledge, competence, or authority, the laity are entitled, and indeed sometimes duty-bound, to express their opinion on matters which concern the good of the Church" (*Lumen Gentium*, 37).

Other Ecclesial Communities

There is an intriguing sentence in Vatican II's document on the Church: "This Church, constituted and organized as a society in the present world, *subsists* in the Catholic Church" (*Lumen Gentium*, 8, emphasis added). If the Council Fathers who wrote this document had intended to say that the Christian Church is *identical with* the Catholic Church, they could have said so. The fact is that they chose not to say this; instead they picked a word that may be read to mean that perhaps the Church of Christ extends beyond the boundaries of the Catholic Church.

The Council even hints that it might be possible to extend the understanding of Church beyond the Catholic Church. The document on the Church says: "The Church has many reasons for knowing that it is joined to the baptized who are honored by the name of Christian, but do not profess the faith in its entirety or have not preserved unity of communion under the successor of Peter" (*Lumen Gentium*, 15). Such groups are described as "churches" or "ecclesiastical communities."

It is worth noting that, while Sacred Scripture has always been an important part of our Christian heritage, it has only been since the Council that the Catholic Church has given due emphasis to it. Until then other Christian "ecclesiastical communities" were much more devoted to the Scriptures than were Catholics.

Infallibility

The Second Vatican Council repeats the teachings of Vatican I on the infallibility, under certain specified conditions, of the college of bishops with the pope or of the pope alone without that college. However, Vatican II adds significantly to our understanding of the Church's infallibility.

It points out that the People of God share in Christ's prophetic office. For this reason "the whole body of the faithful who have received an anointing which comes from the Holy One (see 1 John 2:20 and 27) cannot be mistaken in belief. It shows this characteristic through the entire people's supernatural sense of the faith, when 'from the bishops to the last of the faithful,' it manifests a universal consensus in matters of faith and morals" (*Lumen Gentium*, 12).

Questions for Reflection

1. What does the word *Church* mean to you?
2. How open is your faith community to accepting the responsibilities that come with true collegiality?
3. Lay women and men have an important role in moving forward the Vatican II vision of Church. What are you doing to preserve and promote this vision?

CHAPTER FOUR

Called to be a Sign of Joy and Hope in the World

On December 7, 1965, the Second Vatican Council, in its final session, adopted the Pastoral Constitution on the Church in the Modern World. Its tone and direction differed significantly from the other major documents of Vatican II. In them, the Church had turned inward to shed the light of the gospel on itself to see what God willed it to be. In this new document, the Church looked outward to discover its role in today's world: a world of which it is, after all, a part, but a world that in many ways had ceased to take it seriously.

Partnering With the World

The Church not only looked outward; it did so in a way that no previous Church council had ever done. It looked at the world and smiled, just as God must have smiled when he gazed on the world he had created and saw that it was very good. By contrast, other Church councils had looked at the world and ignored it or deplored it, seeing it as a place of sin and corruption, which they felt compelled to condemn.

Vatican II abandoned this negative mentality about the world outside of the Church: It took the world to its heart in a spirit of concern and compassion. It would partner with the world in discerning "the true signs of God's presence and purpose in the events, needs, and the desires which it shares with the rest of humanity today" (11).

A persistently positive attitude toward that world and an earnest desire to enter into dialogue with it make this document unique in the history of council documents. Its title, "Joy and Hope" (in Latin, *Gaudium et Spes*), and its opening sentence give definite expression to the direction it took and the tone it adopted: "The joys and hopes, the grief and anguish of the people of our time, especially of those who are poor or afflicted, are the joys and hopes, the grief and anguish of the followers of Christ as well. Nothing that is genuinely human fails to find an echo in their hearts" (1).

Witnessing in the Here and Now

To identify what is "genuinely human" in today's world and to discern the Church's role in supporting it are tasks that are essentially incarnational. The Incarnation means that Christ did not redeem the world from afar, but did so by involving himself in the human situation and becoming one of us. This incarnational principle was embraced at the Council and gave birth to a new understanding of the Church's mission.

Before the Council, its mission focused almost exclusively on the "other world" and on assisting individuals to attain eternal salvation. *Gaudium et Spes* moved Catholics toward a new way of thinking that saw the Church's mission as witnessing also to the love and compassion of God in the here and now. Divine love and compassion call us to work for justice, peace, and healing in our globalized world.

The Church has a message for the modern world, but it also has a listening ear and a cooperating heart. It seeks to keep abreast of the changes that are taking place so rapidly in today's world as the human race moves from a more static view of reality to a more dynamic and evolutionary one (5).

Embracing Our Dignity

Gaudium et Spes, the Council's longest document, is in two parts. The first develops its teaching about the vocation of human beings, the world in which they carry this vocation, and the Church's role in helping people live it in today's world. Its four chapters deal with our dignity as human persons, the human community, humanity's activity in the universe, and the role of the Church in the modern world.

The second part focuses on questions and problems of special importance in today's world. Its five chapters deal with the dignity of marriage and the family; the development of culture; economic and social life; the political community; and fostering peace and establishing a community of nations.

Our dignity as humans flows from our creation in the image of God and our call to nothing less than communion with God. The human response to God's call, though personal, is not solitary. Never before in history has it been more urgent to recognize the interdependence of the peoples of the world. Astounding advances in the empirical sciences, in technology, and in the liberal arts have accumulated a vast fund of knowledge.

Seeking Wisdom

The Council reminds us that the present age, more than any other, requires wisdom that can process knowledge and enable us to see that there are radical realities and deep human values that go beyond the immediate, the passing, the superficial. Wisdom helps us to grasp God's providence at work in human history, guiding that history to a fulfillment beyond mere human efforts.

The world's future depends on people endowed with such wisdom. In a significant contrast between the nations of wealth and power and the developing nations, the document states: "It should be pointed out that many nations which are poorer as far as material goods are concerned, yet richer in wisdom, can be of the greatest advantage to others" (15).

At the same time, the Council makes clear its belief in the goodness of human activity in the world. "Far from thinking that what human enterprise and ability have achieved is opposed to God's power as if the rational creature is a rival of the creator, Christians are convinced that the achievements of the human race are a sign of God's greatness and the fulfillment of his mysterious design" (34).

Great progress requires great vigilance. As our power increases, so does our responsibility as individuals and as members of the human community. It should be clear, therefore, that the gospel does not inhibit us from doing all we can for the genuine progress of the human race. On the contrary, it obliges us more strictly to work for everything that contributes in an authentic way to the greater good of humanity.

Responding to Freedom

Human freedom is a wonderful manifestation of the divine image. *Gaudium et Spes*, in its remarkable tribute to human freedom (17), offers a vision unmatched by any previous council. Yet it does not ignore the fact that humans are wounded by sin and need God's grace to orient their freedom toward God.

One of the graces God gives us to guide our freedom is conscience. Conscience, we are told, is "the most secret core and sanctuary of the human person. There they are alone with God whose voice echoes in their depths. By conscience, in a wonderful way, that law is made known which is fulfilled in the love of God and of one's neighbor" (16). Our responsibility to form a correct conscience is something we can hardly achieve without the help of God's grace.

In discussing the existence of atheism in today's world, *Gaudium et Spes* shows a sympathetic understanding of people who espouse it, even suggesting that religious people bear some responsibility for its existence. Poorly instructed Christians may give false impressions of what Christian faith actually teaches about God. The god atheists reject may well be a god that a properly educated Christian would also reject. Likewise, the failure of Christians to live what they say they believe can quickly dry up any interest an atheist might have in learning about the God whom Christians say they worship, but whom they belie by their actions (19).

Sharing Gifts

The laity, as citizens of the world, are especially empowered to bring the Christian message into the marketplace. As an earlier document, the *Dogmatic Constitution on the Church,* said, the laity have the right—even at times the duty—to make known, in areas of their own competence, their opinions on matters which concern the good of the Church.

Part two of *Gaudium et Spes* begins with a section on marriage and the family. Avoiding older terminology that spoke of the primary and secondary purposes of marriage, it insists on the importance of conjugal love. "By its very nature the institution of marriage and married love are ordered to the procreation and education of the offspring and it is in them that it finds its crowning glory" (48). While avoiding the issue of contraception (reserved by Pope Paul VI to a special commission outside the Council), the Council spoke of the importance of responsible parenthood as a decision that married couples—with a properly formed conscience and with due attention to the teaching of the Church—must make in terms of their own good and that of their children (50).

The articles on socioeconomic life echo and develop many of the themes contained in the social encyclicals of the popes from Leo XIII to Paul VI. While space prohibits detailed discussion, one overarching theme is clear: the growing concern about the inequalities between the advanced nations and the developing ones (63).

Several articles are devoted to the promotion of peace and the elimination, or at least the controlling, of the ravages of war.

Peace is not just the absence of war: It is the work of justice. The proliferation of terribly destructive weaponry forces us "to undertake a completely fresh appraisal of war" (80).

The Council adopted the teaching of recent popes in condemning total war and the arms race, though allowing for limited wars of defense, as long as there is no competent international authority with appropriate powers to safeguard peace. It defends the right of conscientious objection to war and praises those who commit themselves to nonviolence. It calls us to join with all peace-loving people in pleading for peace and trying to achieve it (78).

Standing as a Beacon of Light

Gaudium et Spes concludes with a stirring call to all people who love the truth, whatever their culture, race or religion, to join together "to fashion a world better suited to the surpassing dignity of humanity, to strive for a more deeply rooted sense of universal sisterhood and brotherhood, and to meet the pressing appeals of our times with a generous and common effort of love" (91).

Gaudium et Spes was written at the time when the world's peace and security were threatened by the Cold War. Our world today must deal with a deadly terrorism that is often faceless, one that might strike anywhere at any time. In such a situation, the gospel message impels us to put forth every effort to work with people of good will to eliminate conditions that make for terrorism and to work for peace based on justice and freedom.

The Church—confident in the assurance of the Lord Jesus to be with us at all times, even the darkest and seemingly hopeless times—stands as a beacon of light and hope in an otherwise darkening world. *Gaudium et Spes* supports that beacon of light. Its hopes are rooted in the goodness of God, surely, but also in the radical goodness of humanity.

Questions for Reflection

1. In what practical ways is the Catholic Church a sign of joy and hope in the world today?

2. Is your parish living out its mission to be a beacon of light and hope for its members? For citizens of the larger community? What more can be done?

3. How well does the positive attitude toward the world so prevalent in *Gaudium et Spes* match your own? What fears or prejudices do you still need to dispel?

CHAPTER FIVE

Our Compass for the Future

More than fifty years have now passed since the last of the sixteen documents of Vatican II were signed and sent out to the Church. What effect have they had? What value do they still have for us today? In closing out the Jubilee Year 2000, Pope John Paul II spoke of the documents of Vatican II as a great treasure for the Church, a sentiment recently repeated by Pope Benedict XVI. In this chapter, we will begin to explore that treasure.

That Was Then, This Is Now

Vatican II ended in 1965. For a while afterward, everybody commented on how much the Church was changing—how the years after the Council seemed so different from the years before it. The refrain of those who loved all the newness and energy sparked by the Council was: "That was then, this is now." The Mass in Latin, clericalism, a closed Catholic ghetto was *then*, part of our past, described as "pre–Vatican II." Participation in liturgy, parish collaboration, an openness to the world is *now*, part of our future, "post–Vatican II."

Today the focus has shifted. Now the interesting comparison is not so much between the pre–Vatican II period and the post–Vatican II period, but between the time of the Council and our own time. So much has changed in the past fifty years. When those 2,500 bishops gathered in Rome in the early 1960s, the Western world was in the midst of the Cold War, facing Communism and the threat of all-out nuclear war. At the same time, the '60s were about to explode with shock waves of student demonstrations, women's liberation, civil rights movements, and anti-war activism. In the midst of all of this, the Church took up the challenge of updating its enormous institutions—institutions run by a huge corps of clergy and religious.

Today, it is not the Cold War but an open-ended War on Terror that shakes our security. Communism and "the Bomb" have been pushed aside by militant fundamentalism and the threat of weapons of mass destruction. The social movements of the '60s have been replaced by complicated questions about cloning, stem-cell research, and globalization. Now the institutions of the Church are struggling to survive with fewer and fewer priests to run parishes, and with resources—and trust—strained by the sex abuse crisis. And yet, at the same time, lay ministries are flourishing, Catholic colleges are expanding, and parish communities are more active than ever in planning their worship, sharing their faith, and reaching out in service to their neighbors in need.

We might be surprised at how few of the issues that seem so important to us today are found in the documents of Vatican II. We might be tempted to say, "That was then, this is now," and leave the Council texts behind. What makes these documents relevant? What justifies John Paul II's claim that "with the passing of the years, the Council documents have lost nothing of their value or brilliance"?

Behind the pope's confidence may have been his sense that Vatican II offered large principles with lasting value. When we reflect on these larger themes, we see that there is virtually no area of Church life today that is not affected by the Council. If you've ever taken part in a Bible study, witnessed the Easter Vigil liturgy, served on a parish council or as a Eucharistic minister, attended a non-Catholic worship service, reflected on politics in light of your faith, read about a statement from the bishops' conference, picked up the *Catechism of the Catholic Church*, volunteered for a parish service project, been to a funeral, or skimmed a *Catholic Update*, you've experienced the effects of the

Second Vatican Council. The themes of the Council are what help explain to us as a Church where we are today. And, more important, they inspire us to where we can be tomorrow.

More Than a Thick Little Book

Vatican II was an event, a grace-filled moment in the life of the Church. An aging Pope John XXIII caught everyone by surprise when he announced his plans to hold a council. And he surprised everyone again with his opening speech on October 11, 1962. There he publicly disagreed with those "prophets of gloom" around him who saw in the modern world only "prevarication and ruin." Instead, Pope John believed that God is moving humanity to a new order of human relations. The Church needs *aggiornamento*—"updating"—not because the Church feels threatened, but because of its great desire to share the joy of Christ. The pope pointed toward the renewal of the Church with the beautiful words, "It is now only dawn."

By the time the Second Vatican Council closed on December 8, 1965, it had seen two popes, four sessions, and 168 general congregations, or daily meetings. More than 2,500 bishops and other Church leaders took part, 2,212 speeches were delivered, more than 4,300 additional comments were submitted in writing, and more than 1.5 million ballots—deciding everything from formal approval of final documents to individual words in early drafts—were cast. The result was sixteen documents—103,014 words in Latin, six hundred pages in the latest English translation.

Behind these final documents exist a process and a spirit of renewal as important as the texts themselves. Spirit and letter go together. Thus, as important as Vatican II's sixteen documents are, they can never be separated from the spirit of the Council—a spirit of openness to the world and renewal for the Church, a spirit of faithfulness to the past and hope for the future, a spirit, above all, of joy in Christ.

The Four Constitutions

Of the sixteen documents promulgated at Vatican II, four are so foundational that they are designated "constitutions."

Constitution on the Sacred Liturgy. The very first topic the bishops took up at the Council was liturgy. They did so because—of all the draft documents prepared in advance—the one on the liturgy was in the best shape. Many of the ideas for reforming the liturgy had been in the air for some time. Vatican II pulled these ideas together and pushed them forward in a dramatic way.

The Constitution on the Sacred Liturgy boldly declares that the liturgy "is the summit toward which the activity of the Church is directed; it is also the source from which all its power flows" (10). But the liturgy can't be the source and summit if people don't participate in it. Thus the liturgy is to be reformed so as to encourage the "full, conscious, and active" participation of all the faithful (14).

This call to active participation runs throughout the Constitution, guiding its many proposals. In order for people to participate, the liturgy must be easily understood. Vernacular languages should be allowed, rituals should be simplified, and local adaptation should be encouraged. In parishes today, every ritual from baptism to burial has been revised with this one driving concern in mind: That we all actively take part in what God is doing here.

When we celebrated the fortieth anniversary of Vatican II's conclusion, Catholics worldwide celebrated a Year of the Eucharist as a way to nurture this spirit of engagement with the source and summit of our faith.

Dogmatic Constitution on Divine Revelation. After the bishops debated liturgy, they turned to revelation. Unlike the draft on liturgy, the prepared draft on revelation was in poor shape. For a document on the Bible, its language was surprisingly un-biblical, using instead technical terms and philosophical concepts. Moreover, the draft had a very negative tone. Even though it recommended reading the Bible, the text was so full of warnings and cautions that it gave the impression that it was better, in the end, not even to bother.

Thanks in part to the intervention of John XXIII, this draft was sent back to committee for a complete rewrite. The final text of the Constitution speaks of revelation as, above all, a personal interaction between God and humanity: "By this revelation, then, the invisible God, from the fullness of love, addresses men and women as his friends, and lives among them, in order to invite and receive them into his own company" (2). Revelation is not just words about God, it is a living relationship with God.

The *Constitution* recognizes that there is growth in our understanding of revelation. And the whole community has a role to play in handing on the tradition (8). The document acknowledges the contributions of Scripture scholars and points out that Bible passages must be interpreted according to the historical context and literary genres in which they were written. Finally, with great effect on subsequent Church life, the Constitution enthusiastically encourages all the faithful to read the Bible and apply it to their daily lives.

Dogmatic Constitution on the Church. While the debates on liturgy and revelation occupied most of the time at the Council's first session (1962), the document on the Church took up most of the second session (1963). The Dogmatic Constitution on the Church is in many ways the crowning achievement of Vatican II. In it, the Council addressed the nature of the Church itself: Who do we say we are?

Before Vatican II, Catholics might have imagined the Church as something to which they simply belonged. "The Church" then was equated with its structures, its institutions, its hierarchy. But we don't *belong* to the Church; we *are* the Church. The first draft of the Constitution reflected the pre-conciliar mentality. But through successive drafts, revisions were made to affirm more clearly that the Church is not first an institution; it is first of all a mystery bound up in the love of God, "a people made one by the unity of the Father, the Son, and the holy Spirit" (4). The Church is not first the clergy; it is first of all the whole People of God. In fact, the most famous editorial decision of the whole Council was the decision to insert into the Constitution on the Church a chapter—chapter two on the People of God—before the chapter on the hierarchy. The arrangement reflects the theology that we are all the People of God, sharing a oneness and a baptismal equality that precedes the distinctions among different roles in the community.

The People of God theme guides the whole document. The Constitution calls for an increase in shared authority, or collegiality, among the pope and bishops (chapter three). It claims that the laity share fully in the mission of the Church, a claim that has fostered the explosive growth of lay ministries since Vatican II (chapter four). And the document's confidence that everyone in the Church is called to holiness (chapter five) is balanced by its caution that the Church is a pilgrim people, still on the way to the reign of God (chapter seven). Thus, while the outstanding models of holiness we see around us (whether saintly popes or struggling parents) are a sign of the Kingdom "already" arrived, the tragic failures within our Church (such as the sexual abuse of children, discrimination, or indifference) painfully point out the "not yet" reality of our earthly existence.

Pastoral Constitution on the Church in the Modern World. Some of the greatest debates of the third (1964) and fourth (1965) sessions of Vatican II were sparked by the Pastoral Constitution on the Church in the Modern World. The Pastoral Constitution was the only document of the final sixteen that was born during the Council. Near the end of the first session, Cardinal Leon-Joseph Suenens of Belgium addressed his fellow bishops, urging them not just to examine the Church in and of itself. The Council also must examine the Church in relationship to the world at large. This intervention, fully supported by Pope John XXIII, led to the composition of an entirely new document.

The Church in the Modern World begins not with the Bible, liturgy, or doctrine. It begins, in its preface, with the world, with its joys and hopes, grief and anguish. And it underlines the importance of reading the "signs of the times" in order that the Church might respond to the world in which we live (see #4). The document is addressed to all people and expresses hope for dialogue—a dialogue made possible by focusing on the human person. What inspires human hopes? What threatens human life? How is human dignity fostered? What do human communities need? What can human society provide? These are questions that launch a conversation.

The Church offers its own response—a response rooted in faith—but it also listens, engaging the world in dialogue and participating in building up the human family. The five specific areas of concern identified in the Pastoral Constitution remain as important today as they were in 1965: (1) marriage and family, (2) culture, (3) socio-economic life, (4) politics, and (5) peace.

Send in the Spirit

The Council's other documents spell out and apply many of the principles articulated in these four constitutions. Some of these have been more significant than others. But behind them all move the spirit of the Council and the Spirit of Christ—the Spirit who calls all believers to participate actively in the life of faith, who reminds us of God's desire for a personal relationship with humanity, who holds the Church together as the People of God, and who pushes us out into the world to serve.

In his hope-filled vision for the year 2000, Pope John Paul II called the Second Vatican Council the great grace of the twentieth century and the sure compass for the century now beginning.

Questions for Reflection

1. What changes begun at Vatican II have had the greatest impact on the Church? Which will have the greatest impact on the Church's future?

2. Are there some areas where Vatican II went too far? Not far enough?

3. What do you take away from this book regarding your understanding of Vatican II? What are some of the ways this affects your perception of the Church and your role in it?

A Time of New Growth

What is happening in our Church in these opening years of the third millennium? We are something like passengers in an airplane circling above the airport, waiting for the weather to clear so we can see to land.

What happened to the fast rate of change we experienced in those early years after the Council? The pace certainly has slowed. Church leaders seem to have decided that we need to take a break after so much turbulent change. We find ourselves in a time of consolidation and integration, taking stock of where we are.

One might compare the Church to someone experiencing an identity crisis or confusing personal change. Such individuals need time to reflect and "get their act together" before moving on. Maybe the Church leaders sense that it is time for the Church to catch up with itself—to step back a bit and put all the pieces of our fragmented vision into a new whole. This need was satisfied to some degree with the issuing of the *Catechism of the Catholic Church,* but our Vatican II pilgrimage must always move forward.

No matter how carefully we try to put all the truths of the Church into an orderly arrangement, we know we must remain open to new questions needing new answers and to new challenges of growth from the Holy Spirit. Surely new roads lie before us!

We have to ask today, humbly but honestly: Is the vision of the Council being brought to fruition? Is the Church becoming the Church envisioned by the Council? Many would answer with a hesitant and regretful "no" or at least "not anywhere near what it should be."

Surely much has changed in the years since Vatican II. Laypeople are more and more involved in the life of the Church. This is a gain that can never be set back. Yet one cannot help but note the appearance of a strong current of thought and action aimed at gradually recentralizing the Church. More and more authority is being withdrawn from local churches and concentrated in Rome. As one theologian described the way in which things seem to be moving: "The pope is no longer the *ultimate* authority; he is the *only* authority."

Still, the vision of the Council is there, calling us to become the Church that it had hoped would come into being. Laypeople have an important role to play in preserving this vision and moving it forward to fulfillment.

We are still challenged by the work of the Council Fathers, the 2,860 bishops who drafted the Council's sixteen documents. We've been through periods of experimentation, reimagining who we are as Church. Some have decried the changes as too much, too fast; others have complained that the Church isn't changing fast enough.

It has been said that a Church council's vision is not realized until the third generation—two generations after those who held the Council. Our Church today includes adults of this third generation. Those who were at the Council or remember it are fewer and fewer. Those who were children during the Council are split between those who experienced strong Church formation and those whose faith formation was probably, at least initially, lacking in many basics. Many of those born in the mid-1960s and later struggle today to understand their faith in depth.

The momentum behind the Church's ongoing renewal is found in the teachings of Vatican II. It is found in a Church recentered on the Gospels and the Eucharist and in constant dialogue with the world. Pope John Paul II said it best a few years ago: "The best preparation for the new millennium can only be expressed by a renewed commitment *to apply*, as faithfully as possible, the teachings of Vatican II to the life of every individual and of the whole Church" (The Coming Third Millennium, 20).

The Spirit Stays Active

The Holy Spirit, we have been taught, is like the wind. It cannot be boxed in or held in place. We have no idea when the Holy Spirit might tap some new follower of Christ on the shoulder, as happened to Pope John XXIII, and say, "Brother John or Sister Joan, it's time to open more windows; get ready for another Pentecost!"

Does the vision live today? In many people, especially in some glowing centers of liturgy (at times with guns threatening not far away), the emphasis on community, prayer, Scripture, and *peoplehood* has flourished. In others, a strangling fear of change, usually a matter of temperament, inhibits growth. Perennial human apathy plays its part.

But the relentless Spirit of Pentecost is always working—everywhere, not just where things appear bright. It is working, too, perhaps even more relentlessly, in the night of persecution, apparent failure and spiritual change. God works in seconds—and centuries. Perhaps the full impact of the Council is yet to come.

Sources

Feister, John, and Jack Wintz, O.F.M. "Road Map for the Future: Teachings of Vatican II," *Vatican II Today*, March 2004.

Foley, Leonard, O.F.M. "Vatican II: The Vision Lives On," *Catholic Update*, March 1993.

Hahnenberg, Edward P. "Treasures of Vatican II: Our Compass for the Future," *Catholic Update*, September 2005.

Shannon, William H. "Today's Church: A Look in the Mirror," *Vatican II Today*, November 2004.

———. "Our Church: Called to Be a Sign of Joy and Hope," *Vatican II Today*, December 2004.

Wintz, Jack, O.F.M. "Seven Key Trends in the Church Today," *Catholic Update*, January 1998.

Contributors

John Feister is editor-in-chief of *St. Anthony Messenger* magazine. He has master's degrees in humanities and theology from Xavier University in Cincinnati, Ohio.

Leonard Foley, O.F.M., was the editor of *St. Anthony Messenger* magazine and the author of the bestselling *Believing in Jesus: A Popular Overview of the Catholic Faith.*

Edward P. Hahnenberg, Ph.D., is the author of *A Concise Guide to the Documents of Vatican II* and *Ministries: A Relational Approach.* He is the inaugural holder of the Jack and Mary Jane Breen Chair in Catholic Systematic Theology at John Carroll University.

William H. Shannon, was the founding president of the International Thomas Merton Society and the author of numerous *Catholic Update* newsletters, *Thomas Merton: An Introduction,* and *Exploring the Catechism of the Catholic Church.*

Jack Wintz, O.F.M., is senior editor of *Catholic Update* and editor emeritus of *St. Anthony Messenger* magazine. He is the author of *St. Anthony: His Life, Legends, and Devotions, Friar Jack's Favorite Prayers* and *Friar Jack's E-spirations.*